TRAVLE TO
KOH SAMET

Traveler's Handbook

Joanne F. Sturges

All rights reserved. No part of this publication may be reproduced, distributed, or transmitted in any form or by any means, including photocopying, recording, or other electronic or mechanical methods, without the prior written permission of the publisher, except in the case of brief quotations embodied in critical reviews and certain other noncommercial uses permitted by copyright law.

Copyright © Joanne F. Sturges, 2023

Table of content

INTRODUCTION
About Koh Samet
Geography and Location of Koh Samet
Brief History of Koh Samet
Getting to Koh Samet
Transportation Options on Koh Samet
Arrival and Departure on Koh Samet
Sai Kaew Beach
Ao Phai Beach
Ao Wong Duean Beach
Ao Hin Khok Beach
Ao Nuan Beach
Ao Cho Beach
Ao Wai Beach
Ao Lung Dam Beach
Activities and Attractions
Water Sports and Diving
Snorkeling Spots
Hiking and Nature Trails
Sunset Viewpoints
Boat Tours and Island Hopping
Dining and Nightlife
Popular Restaurants and Cafes
Nightlife and Entertainment Options
Accommodation Options

Resorts and Hotel
Budget and Backpacker Accommodations
Beachfront Bungalows
Local Culture and Festivals
Traditional Thai Customs
Festivals and Celebrations
Practical Information
Weather and Best Time to Visit
Money and Currency Exchange
Safety Tips
Health and Medical Facilities
Communication and Internet Access
Exploring Nearby Islands and Attractions
Koh Chang
Koh Kood
Rayong City
Conclusion

INTRODUCTION

Welcome to the enchanting island of Koh Samet! Nestled in the Gulf of Thailand, Koh Samet is a tropical paradise known for its pristine beaches, crystal-clear waters, and laid-back atmosphere. Whether you're seeking relaxation under swaying palm trees, thrilling water sports adventures, or vibrant nightlife, Koh Samet has something for everyone.

In this book, we will take you on a virtual journey to explore the beauty and wonders of Koh Samet. You'll discover the island's rich history, its stunning beaches, and the plethora of activities and attractions that await you. We'll provide you with essential information on how to get to Koh Samet, the best times to visit, and practical tips to make your stay enjoyable.

From the bustling shores of Sai Kaew Beach to the hidden gems of Ao Phai Beach, we'll guide you through the different beaches that adorn the coastline of Koh Samet. Immerse yourself in the vibrant marine life as we delve into the world of snorkeling and diving spots that showcase the island's underwater treasures.

But Koh Samet is not just about sun-soaked shores. We'll also take you on an adventure inland, where you can explore lush jungles, discover hidden waterfalls, and embark on exhilarating hikes. And when the sun sets, we'll show you the best dining options to savor mouthwatering Thai cuisine and reveal the hotspots for a night of fun and entertainment.

Throughout this book, we'll provide practical information to help you plan your trip, including transportation options, accommodation choices, and insights into local customs and festivals. You'll also find recommendations for nearby islands and attractions if you wish to extend your adventure beyond Koh Samet's shores.

So, grab your sunscreen, pack your beach essentials, and get ready to embark on an unforgettable journey to Koh Samet. Let this book be your ultimate guide as you explore the beauty, tranquility, and vibrant energy of this remarkable island.

About Koh Samet

Koh Samet, also spelled as Ko Samet or Koh Samed, is a small island located in the Gulf of Thailand, approximately 200 kilometers southeast of Bangkok. It is part of the Rayong Province and is a popular destination for both local Thai and international tourists.

The island covers an area of about 6.5 square kilometers and boasts beautiful white sandy beaches, crystal-clear turquoise waters, and lush tropical vegetation. One of the reasons Koh Samet is so appealing is its proximity to Bangkok, making it easily accessible for a weekend getaway or a longer vacation.

The island's charm lies in its laid-back atmosphere and natural beauty. Unlike some of the more developed Thai islands, Koh Samet has managed to maintain its tranquil ambiance, making it an ideal destination for those seeking relaxation and a slower pace of life.

Koh Samet is known for its stunning beaches, each with its own unique character. Sai Kaew Beach is the most popular and bustling beach, offering a wide range of water sports, beachside bars, and restaurants. Ao Phai Beach is another lively spot, known for its vibrant nightlife and beach parties. For those seeking a quieter beach experience, Ao Wong Duean and Ao Hin Khok offer a more serene and peaceful ambiance.

In addition to its beautiful beaches, Koh Samet is home to a variety of marine life, making it a haven for snorkelers and divers. The clear waters provide excellent visibility, and the coral reefs teem with colorful fish and other fascinating underwater creatures. There are diving centers on the island that offer courses and excursions for both beginners and experienced divers.

Koh Samet also offers opportunities for exploration beyond its beaches. The island is dotted with hiking trails that lead to viewpoints overlooking the stunning coastline and surrounding islands. Inland, you can discover hidden waterfalls, tropical forests, and wildlife.

The island has a range of accommodations to suit different budgets and preferences, including luxury resorts, beachfront bungalows, and budget-friendly guesthouses. There are also numerous restaurants and beachside eateries where you can sample delicious Thai cuisine, fresh seafood, and international dishes.

Whether you're seeking a tranquil beach retreat, an adventure in nature, or a lively beach party scene, Koh Samet offers a perfect blend of natural beauty, relaxation, and entertainment. It's a place where you can unwind, soak up the sun, and immerse yourself in the tropical paradise that is Koh Samet.

Geography and Location of Koh Samet

Koh Samet is situated in the Gulf of Thailand, off the eastern coast of Thailand. It is part of the Rayong

Province, which is located approximately 200 kilometers southeast of the capital city, Bangkok.

The island is relatively small, covering an area of about 6.5 square kilometers (2.5 square miles). It has a roughly oval shape, stretching about 6.5 kilometers (4 miles) from north to south and 3.5 kilometers (2.2 miles) from east to west.

Koh Samet is part of the Khao Laem Ya-Mu Ko Samet National Park, which includes the island itself and the surrounding waters. The national park was established in 1981 to preserve the island's natural beauty, marine life, and ecological diversity.

The island is characterized by its sandy beaches, picturesque bays, and rocky headlands. The coastline is dotted with a variety of beaches, each with its own distinct features and atmosphere. The eastern side of the island, facing the Gulf of Thailand, tends to have calmer waters and more extensive sandy beaches, while the western side is characterized by rocky outcrops and quieter bays.

Koh Samet is located close to the mainland, and there are several piers in the town of Ban Phe from where visitors can catch ferry or speedboat services to the island. The journey from Ban Phe to Koh Samet typically takes around 30 minutes to an hour, depending on the type of boat and sea conditions.

The island's strategic location in the Gulf of Thailand makes it easily accessible from various major cities in Thailand. Bangkok's Suvarnabhumi Airport is the nearest international airport, and from there, it is a convenient journey to Koh Samet by road or ferry.

The geographical location of Koh Samet contributes to its popularity as a weekend getaway or a short vacation spot for both local residents and international travelers.

Its proximity to Bangkok, combined with its natural beauty and relaxed atmosphere, makes it an attractive destination for those seeking a tropical island experience without venturing too far from the mainland.

Brief History of Koh Samet

Koh Samet has a rich history that dates back centuries. The island's name, "Samet," means "cajeput tree" in Thai, which is a type of evergreen tree that is native to the region. The island was named after the abundance of cajeput trees found on its shores.

Historical records indicate that Koh Samet was once inhabited by the indigenous sea gypsies, known as the "Chao Ley" or Moken people. These nomadic fishermen lived in harmony with the sea and relied on its resources for their sustenance.

During the Ayutthaya Kingdom period (1351-1767), Koh Samet served as a safe haven for ships seeking shelter from storms or pirates. It was an important anchorage point and a strategic location for maritime trade between Ayutthaya (the capital at the time) and other neighboring countries.

In the late 19th century, during the reign of King Rama V (King Chulalongkorn), Koh Samet came under the control of the Royal Forest Department, which recognized the island's ecological significance and took steps to protect its natural resources.

In more recent history, during the Vietnam War in the 1960s and 1970s, Koh Samet served as a recreational spot for American soldiers stationed in Thailand. Its beautiful beaches and proximity to military bases made it a popular destination for relaxation and downtime.

In 1981, Koh Samet was designated as part of the Khao Laem Ya-Mu Ko Samet National Park, recognizing its ecological importance and preserving its natural beauty. The national park status has helped protect the island's ecosystems and wildlife, ensuring its sustainability for future generations.

Over the years, Koh Samet has experienced increased tourism development, with the construction of resorts, hotels, and other amenities to accommodate the growing number of visitors. However, efforts have been made to strike a balance between tourism and conservation to maintain the island's charm and natural integrity.

Today, Koh Samet continues to be a popular tourist destination, attracting visitors from around the world who come to enjoy its pristine beaches, turquoise waters, and laid-back atmosphere. Its history, natural beauty, and vibrant culture make it a captivating destination for those seeking a tropical island experience in Thailand.

Getting to Koh Samet

Koh Samet is easily accessible from Bangkok and other major cities in Thailand. Here are the common transportation options to reach the island:

1. By Car/Taxi: From Bangkok, you can take a taxi or drive to the coastal town of Ban Phe, which is the main gateway to Koh Samet. The journey takes approximately 2-3 hours, depending on traffic conditions. Once you reach Ban Phe, you can park your car in one of the designated parking areas and proceed to the piers to catch a ferry or speedboat to the island.
2. By Public Bus: Regular buses operate between Bangkok's Eastern Bus Terminal (Ekkamai) and Ban Phe. The journey takes about 3-4 hours,

depending on traffic. From Ban Phe, you can proceed to the piers to catch a boat to Koh Samet.
3. By Minivan: Minivan services are available from various locations in Bangkok to Ban Phe. These minivans provide a more direct and faster option compared to buses, typically taking around 2-3 hours. Again, once you arrive in Ban Phe, you can head to the piers for onward transportation to Koh Samet.
4. By Ferry/Speedboat: Ban Phe has several piers from where you can catch a ferry or speedboat to Koh Samet. The ferry journey takes around 30 minutes to an hour, depending on the type of boat and sea conditions. Speedboats are a faster option, usually taking about 15-20 minutes. The boat services operate from early morning until late afternoon or early evening, with more frequent departures during peak season.

It's important to note that there are multiple piers in Ban Phe, including Nuanthip Pier, Sri Ban Phe Pier, and Nadan Pier. The choice of pier may depend on the boat operator you select or the specific beach on Koh Samet you wish to reach. Most boat services provide transportation directly to the main beaches on the island.

Tickets for the ferry or speedboat can be purchased at the piers, and prices may vary slightly between operators. It's advisable to check the schedules and fares in advance, especially during high season or holiday periods, to ensure smooth travel arrangements.

Once you arrive at Koh Samet, you will be greeted by the beauty of the island's beaches and can proceed to your chosen accommodation via local transportation options such as songthaews (shared taxis) or private taxis, which are available near the piers.

Remember to plan your return journey in advance, considering the boat schedules and allowing sufficient time to reach the mainland for your onward travel arrangements.

Transportation Options on Koh Samet

Once you arrive on Koh Samet, there are various transportation options available to explore the island and move between its different beaches and attractions. Here are the common modes of transportation on Koh Samet:

1. Walking: Many of the main beaches and attractions on Koh Samet are within walking distance of each other. If you prefer a leisurely pace and want to enjoy the island's scenic beauty, walking is a convenient option. It allows you to explore the beaches, find hidden spots, and take in the tranquil atmosphere at your own pace.
2. Songthaews: Songthaews are the most common form of public transportation on the island. These open-air pickup trucks with bench seating in the back operate as shared taxis. They follow specific routes and can take you from one beach to another or to popular spots on the island. Songthaews usually display signs indicating the destination or route they serve. Just wave one down, hop on, and let the driver know your

destination. Fare prices are usually fixed, so it's a good idea to confirm the price before getting on board.

3. Motorcycle Taxis: Motorcycle taxis, locally known as "motorsai," are another popular option for getting around Koh Samet. Riders typically wear brightly colored vests and can be found near the piers and major beaches. Motorcycle taxis are a convenient and quick way to navigate the island, especially if you're carrying luggage or want to reach specific locations faster. Negotiate the fare with the rider before hopping on, and make sure to wear a helmet for safety.

4. Bicycle Rentals: Renting a bicycle is a popular choice for exploring Koh Samet, especially for those who enjoy a more active and eco-friendly experience. You can find bicycle rental shops near the main beaches or in the town area. Renting a bicycle allows you the freedom to explore the island at your own pace, discovering hidden beaches, scenic viewpoints, and local attractions.

5. Motorbike Rentals: For more independent exploration, renting a motorbike is an option. Motorbike rentals are available on the island, and they offer greater flexibility in terms of destinations and timings. However, it's essential to have prior experience riding a motorbike, wear

a helmet, and observe traffic rules and safety precautions. Be sure to check the condition of the bike before renting, and remember that some beaches may have limited parking facilities.

It's important to note that cars are not allowed on Koh Samet, as the island aims to preserve its natural environment and minimize congestion.

Choosing the right transportation option depends on your preferences, budget, and the locations you plan to visit on the island. Consider the distance, time, and convenience when deciding which mode of transportation suits your needs. Regardless of your choice, exploring Koh Samet is a delightful experience, as the island is relatively small and offers a relaxed and picturesque environment for travelers to enjoy.

Arrival and Departure on Koh Samet

When arriving on Koh Samet, as a visitor, you will typically arrive at one of the piers located in the town of Ban Phe on the mainland. Here's what you can expect during your arrival and departure on Koh Samet:

Arrival:

1. Pier Arrival: Upon reaching the designated pier in Ban Phe, you will disembark from the ferry or speedboat. The pier area is usually bustling with activity, with vendors, transportation services, and local agents offering assistance and information.
2. Admission Fee: Before boarding the boat to Koh Samet, you may be required to pay a small admission fee for entry into the Khao Laem Ya-Mu Ko Samet National Park, as the island is part of the protected area. The fee helps support the conservation efforts on the island.

3. Local Transportation: After disembarking, you will find local transportation options such as songthaews (shared taxis) and motorcycle taxis near the pier. They can take you to your desired beach or accommodation on Koh Samet. Agree on the fare with the driver before setting off, and keep in mind that some accommodations may provide shuttle services.

Departure:

1. Boat Departure: As your time on Koh Samet comes to an end, you will need to make your way back to the pier for your departure. Plan your departure time in advance to ensure you have enough time to catch your chosen boat service.
2. Boat Schedules: Boat services from Koh Samet to Ban Phe usually operate from early morning until late afternoon or early evening. However, it's recommended to check the boat schedules in advance, as they may vary depending on the season, weather conditions, and demand.
3. Ticket Purchase: At the pier on Koh Samet, you can purchase tickets for the ferry or speedboat back to the mainland. Prices may vary slightly between operators, so compare options and choose a reliable and reputable service. It's advisable to purchase your tickets a little earlier

to secure your preferred departure time, especially during peak season or busy periods.
4. Return Transportation: To reach the pier from your accommodation, you can use the same local transportation options mentioned earlier, such as songthaews or motorcycle taxis. Allow sufficient time for the journey to the pier, considering any possible traffic or delays.

It's important to note that boat services can be affected by weather conditions, especially during the rainy season or in case of strong winds. In such instances, boat schedules may be altered or temporarily suspended for safety reasons. It's recommended to check weather forecasts and boat operations updates if you are traveling during unpredictable weather.

By following these guidelines, you can ensure a smooth arrival and departure experience on Koh Samet, allowing you to make the most of your time on this picturesque island.

Exploring the Beaches of Koh Samet

Koh Samet is renowned for its beautiful beaches, each offering its own unique charm and atmosphere. Here are some of the beaches you can explore on the island:

1. Sai Kaew Beach: Sai Kaew Beach, also known as Diamond Beach, is the most popular and longest beach on Koh Samet. It features a wide stretch of powdery white sand and offers a variety of water activities such as jet skiing, banana boat rides, and snorkeling. The beach is lined with resorts, beachfront restaurants, and bars, making it a vibrant and lively spot both during the day and at night.
2. Ao Phai Beach: Ao Phai Beach is a lively and bustling beach known for its nightlife and beach parties. It offers a vibrant atmosphere with beachfront bars, restaurants, and music. During the day, you can relax on the sandy beach, soak up the sun, and enjoy the crystal-clear waters. In

the evening, the beach comes alive with beach parties and fire shows.

3. Ao Wong Duean: Ao Wong Duean is a picturesque beach with soft white sand and calm turquoise waters. It offers a more tranquil and laid-back ambiance compared to the busier beaches. The beach is fringed with palm trees, providing shade for sunbathers. There are several beachfront resorts, restaurants, and massage services available, making it an ideal spot for relaxation and rejuvenation.

4. Ao Hin Khok: Ao Hin Khok, also known as the Quiet Bay, lives up to its name as a serene and peaceful beach. It is a secluded spot with a tranquil atmosphere, making it a great option for those seeking a quieter beach experience. The beach is less crowded and offers a relaxed setting for sunbathing, swimming, and enjoying the natural beauty of the surroundings.

5. Ao Nuan: Ao Nuan is a smaller and lesser-known beach tucked away in a picturesque bay. It is a hidden gem with calm waters and a peaceful atmosphere. The beach is surrounded by lush greenery, giving it a secluded and intimate feel. Ao Nuan is an excellent choice for snorkeling, as the waters are teeming with marine life and colorful coral reefs.

These are just a few examples of the beautiful beaches you can explore on Koh Samet. Each beach has its own distinct character and offerings, allowing you to choose the atmosphere that suits your preferences. Whether you're looking for a lively beach with water activities and nightlife or a serene spot for relaxation and tranquility, Koh Samet's beaches have something to offer for everyone.

Sai Kaew Beach

Sai Kaew Beach, also known as Diamond Beach, is one of the most popular and vibrant beaches on Koh Samet. Here's what you can expect when exploring Sai Kaew Beach:

1. Beach Activities: Sai Kaew Beach offers a wide range of activities to keep visitors entertained. You can enjoy swimming in the clear turquoise waters or simply relax on the soft white sand.

The beach is well-equipped with water sports facilities, including jet skis, banana boat rides, and kayaks, allowing you to have fun in the water.
2. Beachfront Facilities: The beach is lined with resorts, hotels, and beachfront restaurants, offering a variety of amenities and services. You'll find beach chairs and umbrellas available for rent, providing comfortable spots to relax and soak up the sun. There are also massage services available on the beach, allowing you to indulge in a relaxing beachside massage.
3. Dining and Nightlife: Sai Kaew Beach is known for its vibrant dining and nightlife scene. Along the beachfront, you'll find a wide selection of restaurants and bars offering both Thai and international cuisine. You can enjoy a delicious seafood dinner while taking in the beautiful ocean views. In the evenings, the beach comes alive with beach parties, live music, and fire shows, providing a lively atmosphere for those seeking nighttime entertainment.
4. Shopping: Sai Kaew Beach has a variety of shops and vendors selling beachwear, souvenirs, and other items. You can stroll along the beach and browse through the shops to find unique gifts or essentials for your beach vacation.

5. Excursions and Tours: Sai Kaew Beach serves as a convenient starting point for various excursions and tours around the island. You can book boat trips to explore nearby islands, go snorkeling or scuba diving in the vibrant underwater world, or take a tour to visit other attractions on Koh Samet.

It's worth noting that Sai Kaew Beach can get busy, especially during peak tourist seasons. If you prefer a quieter beach experience, it's advisable to visit early in the morning or during weekdays when it's less crowded.

Sai Kaew Beach's combination of beautiful sandy shores, crystal-clear waters, water sports activities, beachfront amenities, and vibrant atmosphere make it a popular choice among travelers looking for a lively beach experience on Koh Samet.

Ao Phai Beach

Ao Phai Beach is another popular beach on Koh Samet, known for its lively atmosphere and vibrant nightlife. Here's what you can expect when exploring Ao Phai Beach:

1. Beach Activities: Ao Phai Beach offers a range of activities for beachgoers. You can swim in the inviting turquoise waters, sunbathe on the soft sandy beach, or simply relax under the shade of the palm trees. The beach is also a great spot for snorkeling, allowing you to discover the colorful marine life and coral reefs.
2. Beachfront Entertainment: Ao Phai Beach is known for its lively beachfront entertainment. You'll find a variety of beach bars, restaurants, and lounges offering drinks, music, and delicious food. During the day, you can enjoy refreshing cocktails and tasty snacks while lounging on beach chairs. In the evening, the beach comes alive with vibrant beach parties, fire shows, and live music, creating an energetic and fun-filled atmosphere.
3. Watersports: If you're seeking adventure, Ao Phai Beach has plenty of watersports activities to offer. You can try your hand at jet skiing, parasailing, or take a thrilling ride on a banana

boat. Rental shops along the beach provide equipment and instruction for these exciting water-based activities.

4. Dining Options: Ao Phai Beach boasts a wide array of dining options to satisfy your cravings. From beachfront seafood restaurants to international cuisine, you'll find a variety of choices to suit your taste. Indulge in fresh seafood dishes, traditional Thai delicacies, or international favorites while enjoying the picturesque beach views.

5. Nightlife: Ao Phai Beach is known for its vibrant nightlife scene. The beach bars and clubs come alive after dark, offering a mix of live music, DJs, and beach parties. You can dance the night away with fellow travelers and enjoy the lively atmosphere that makes Ao Phai Beach a popular destination for nightlife enthusiasts.

It's important to note that due to its popularity and lively atmosphere, Ao Phai Beach can be crowded, especially during weekends and peak tourist seasons. If you prefer a more tranquil beach experience, it's advisable to visit during weekdays or choose other beaches on the island.

Ao Phai Beach's combination of exciting watersports, beachfront entertainment, dining options, and vibrant nightlife makes it an excellent choice for those seeking a lively and energetic beach experience on Koh Samet.

Ao Wong Duean Beach

Ao Wong Duean Beach is a picturesque and tranquil beach on Koh Samet, known for its natural beauty and relaxing ambiance. Here's what you can expect when exploring Ao Wong Duean Beach:

1. Scenic Beauty: Ao Wong Duean Beach is celebrated for its stunning natural surroundings. It features soft white sand, crystal-clear waters, and a backdrop of lush greenery. The beach is fringed with swaying palm trees, providing shade and creating a serene and tropical atmosphere. The pristine waters are perfect for swimming and cooling off from the warm Thai sun.
2. Peaceful Atmosphere: Compared to the busier and more crowded beaches on Koh Samet, Ao

Wong Duean offers a more peaceful and laid-back environment. It's an ideal spot for relaxation and tranquility, away from the hustle and bustle. The calm waters and tranquil setting make it a favorite among couples, families, and those seeking a quieter beach experience.

3. Beachfront Amenities: Despite its peaceful setting, Ao Wong Duean Beach still offers a range of amenities and facilities. You'll find beachfront resorts, restaurants, and bars that provide comfortable seating, beach chairs, and umbrellas. You can relax and enjoy the beach while savoring delicious meals and refreshing drinks.
4. Snorkeling: Ao Wong Duean Beach is also a great place for snorkeling enthusiasts. The clear waters near the rocks at either end of the beach offer an opportunity to explore the vibrant marine life. Grab a snorkeling mask and snorkel and venture out to discover colorful coral reefs and tropical fish.
5. Sunset Views: One of the highlights of Ao Wong Duean Beach is the stunning sunset views. As the day draws to a close, the beach becomes even more enchanting. Watching the sun dip below the horizon and painting the sky in a kaleidoscope of colors is a magical experience. Find a cozy spot

on the beach, sit back, and soak in the breathtaking sunset views.

It's important to note that although Ao Wong Duean Beach is quieter compared to some of the more popular beaches, it still attracts visitors, especially during peak tourist seasons. If you prefer a more secluded experience, consider visiting early in the morning or during weekdays.

Ao Wong Duean Beach's natural beauty, peaceful atmosphere, and opportunities for relaxation and snorkeling make it an excellent choice for those seeking a serene and idyllic beach experience on Koh Samet.

Ao Hin Khok Beach

Ao Hin Khok, also known as the Quiet Bay, is a secluded and serene beach on Koh Samet. Here's what you can expect when exploring Ao Hin Khok Beach:

1. Tranquil Atmosphere: As the name suggests, Ao Hin Khok offers a tranquil and peaceful setting away from the crowds. The beach is less frequented by tourists, providing a quieter and more secluded experience compared to some of the more popular beaches on the island. It's an ideal spot for those seeking relaxation and solitude.
2. Serene Natural Beauty: Ao Hin Khok Beach is known for its natural beauty and pristine surroundings. The beach features soft white sand and crystal-clear waters, inviting visitors to unwind and enjoy the scenic views. The absence of beachfront developments and the lush greenery surrounding the bay create a serene and unspoiled atmosphere.
3. Privacy and Seclusion: Due to its secluded location, Ao Hin Khok offers a greater sense of privacy. You can find a quiet spot on the beach to relax, read a book, or simply soak up the sun without disturbances. It's an excellent option for couples, families, or anyone looking for a peaceful beach experience.

4. Swimming and Sunbathing: The calm and gentle waters of Ao Hin Khok Beach make it suitable for swimming. You can take a refreshing dip in the clear waters or simply lounge on the beach and enjoy the tranquil atmosphere. The soft sand is perfect for sunbathing, and the natural shade from the surrounding trees provides relief from the sun.
5. Nature Exploration: Besides relaxing on the beach, Ao Hin Khok also offers opportunities for nature exploration. You can take a leisurely stroll along the shoreline and admire the scenic beauty of the area. The beach is also close to hiking trails that lead to viewpoints with panoramic vistas of the island.

It's important to note that due to its secluded nature, there are limited facilities and amenities available on Ao Hin Khok Beach. It's advisable to bring your own essentials such as water, snacks, and beach equipment if you plan to spend an extended period there.

Ao Hin Khok Beach's serene ambiance, unspoiled beauty, and sense of privacy make it an excellent choice for those seeking a quiet and secluded beach experience on Koh Samet.

Ao Nuan Beach

Ao Nuan Beach is a smaller and lesser-known beach on Koh Samet, offering a tranquil and intimate setting for visitors. Here's what you can expect when exploring Ao Nuan Beach:

1. Secluded and Intimate Atmosphere: Ao Nuan Beach is tucked away in a picturesque bay, providing a secluded and intimate beach experience. It is less crowded compared to some of the more popular beaches on the island, making it a great choice for those seeking a peaceful and tranquil environment.
2. Pristine Natural Beauty: The beach boasts soft white sand and clear turquoise waters, creating a beautiful and pristine setting. The calm and shallow waters are ideal for swimming and wading. The beach is surrounded by lush

greenery and rocks, adding to the natural charm of the area.
3. Snorkeling Opportunities: Ao Nuan Beach is known for its excellent snorkeling opportunities. The waters around the beach are home to colorful coral reefs and diverse marine life. Snorkelers can explore the underwater world and witness the vibrant marine ecosystem up close.
4. Relaxation and Sunbathing: Ao Nuan Beach provides a peaceful and serene environment for relaxation. You can find a quiet spot on the beach, lay down a towel, and bask in the sun while listening to the gentle sound of the waves. The natural shade from the surrounding trees offers a respite from the sun's rays.
5. Beachfront Refreshments: Although smaller in size, Ao Nuan Beach does have a small beachfront restaurant where you can enjoy refreshments and light snacks. You can savor delicious Thai dishes and refreshing drinks while taking in the tranquil atmosphere of the beach.

It's important to note that Ao Nuan Beach is relatively secluded and may not have extensive facilities or amenities compared to more popular beaches on the island. It's advisable to bring your own beach essentials such as water, snacks, and sunscreen.

Ao Nuan Beach's secluded and intimate ambiance, pristine beauty, and snorkeling opportunities make it an excellent choice for those seeking a peaceful and immersive beach experience on Koh Samet.

Ao Cho Beach

Ao Cho Beach is a charming and picturesque beach on Koh Samet, known for its tranquil atmosphere and natural beauty. Here's what you can expect when exploring Ao Cho Beach:

1. Serene and Relaxing Atmosphere: Ao Cho Beach offers a serene and relaxing environment, making it an ideal spot for those seeking tranquility. The beach is less crowded compared to some of the more popular beaches on the island, allowing visitors to enjoy a peaceful and laid-back experience.

2. Soft Sand and Clear Waters: The beach features soft, powdery white sand and clear turquoise waters. You can take a leisurely stroll along the shore, feeling the soft sand beneath your feet. The calm and gentle waters are perfect for swimming and cooling off in the tropical heat.
3. Lush Greenery and Natural Surroundings: Ao Cho Beach is surrounded by lush greenery, providing a beautiful backdrop for your beach experience. The area is rich in tropical vegetation, creating a natural and scenic setting that adds to the charm of the beach.
4. Beachfront Restaurants and Bars: Along the beach, you'll find a selection of beachfront restaurants and bars. These establishments offer a variety of local Thai cuisine, fresh seafood, and refreshing beverages. You can savor delicious meals while enjoying the stunning views of the beach and the ocean.
5. Relaxation and Sunbathing: Ao Cho Beach provides ample space for relaxation and sunbathing. You can find a comfortable spot on the beach, lay down your towel, and soak up the sun's rays. The calm atmosphere and gentle sea breeze make it an ideal place to unwind and recharge.
6. Water Activities: While Ao Cho Beach may not offer as many water activities as some other

beaches on the island, you can still enjoy swimming and snorkeling in the clear waters. You can bring your snorkeling gear and explore the underwater world, observing colorful marine life and coral reefs.

It's worth noting that Ao Cho Beach may have limited facilities compared to larger and more developed beaches. It's recommended to bring your own beach essentials, such as towels, sunscreen, and water, for a comfortable and enjoyable beach outing.

Ao Cho Beach's serene ambiance, natural beauty, and tranquil atmosphere make it a great choice for those seeking a peaceful and relaxing beach experience on Koh Samet.

Ao Wai Beach

Ao Wai Beach is a secluded and idyllic beach on Koh Samet, offering a serene and peaceful atmosphere. Here's what you can expect when exploring Ao Wai Beach:

1. Secluded and Tranquil Setting: Ao Wai Beach is tucked away in a quiet cove, providing a secluded and intimate beach experience. The beach is less crowded compared to some of the more popular beaches on the island, making it a perfect choice for those seeking privacy and tranquility.
2. Pristine Natural Beauty: The beach boasts soft white sand, clear turquoise waters, and a backdrop of lush greenery. The tranquil setting and untouched natural beauty of Ao Wai create a serene and picturesque environment. It's a great spot to relax, unwind, and enjoy the beauty of the surrounding nature.
3. Swimming and Snorkeling: The calm and shallow waters of Ao Wai Beach are ideal for swimming and snorkeling. You can take a refreshing dip in the crystal-clear waters or grab your snorkeling gear to explore the underwater world. The area near the rocks at either end of the

beach is particularly good for snorkeling, as it offers opportunities to observe colorful marine life and coral reefs.

4. Beachfront Relaxation: Ao Wai Beach provides ample space for relaxation and sunbathing. You can find a quiet spot on the soft sand, set up your beach towel, and enjoy the gentle sea breeze. The natural shade from the surrounding trees offers a peaceful respite from the sun, creating a comfortable environment for unwinding.

5. Limited Facilities: It's important to note that Ao Wai Beach has limited facilities compared to more developed beaches. There are a few beachfront accommodations and restaurants, but they may be smaller in scale. It's advisable to bring your own essentials such as water, snacks, and sunscreen when visiting Ao Wai.

The secluded and serene atmosphere, pristine natural beauty, and opportunities for swimming and snorkeling make Ao Wai Beach a hidden gem for those seeking a peaceful and unspoiled beach experience on Koh Samet.

Ao Lung Dam Beach

I apologize, but I couldn't find any information about "Ao Lung Dam Beach" on Koh Samet or any other known beach destinations. It's possible that the name might be misspelled or referring to a lesser-known or unofficial beach. Koh Samet is home to several beautiful beaches, but "Ao Lung Dam Beach" doesn't appear to be one of them. If you have any other questions or need information about other beaches or topics, feel free to ask.

Activities and Attractions

Koh Samet offers a variety of activities and attractions for visitors to enjoy. Here are some popular options:

1. Beach Activities: The beaches of Koh Samet are perfect for a wide range of activities. You can swim in the clear waters, relax on the sandy shores, sunbathe under the tropical sun, or build sandcastles with your family. Many beaches also

offer water sports such as jet skiing, kayaking, paddleboarding, and banana boat rides.
2. Snorkeling and Diving: Koh Samet is surrounded by beautiful coral reefs and marine life, making it an excellent destination for snorkeling and diving enthusiasts. Explore the underwater world and discover colorful fish, vibrant corals, and other fascinating marine creatures. There are several dive shops on the island that offer snorkeling and diving trips.
3. Island Hopping: Koh Samet is part of the Rayong Province, which includes many other nearby islands and islets. You can embark on an island hopping tour to explore these scenic islands, such as Koh Kudi, Koh Talu, or Koh Thalu. Enjoy pristine beaches, clear waters, and breathtaking views as you hop from one island to another.
4. Sunset Watching: Koh Samet is known for its stunning sunsets. Head to one of the western-facing beaches, such as Sai Kaew Beach or Ao Prao Beach, and witness the mesmerizing sight of the sun setting over the horizon. It's a magical experience and a great opportunity for beautiful photographs.
5. National Park Exploration: Koh Samet is home to Khao Laem Ya-Mu Ko Samet National Park, which covers both land and sea areas. Take a hike to Khao Laem Ya, the highest point on the island,

and enjoy panoramic views of the surrounding islands and coastline. The national park also offers nature trails, viewpoints, and picnic areas for visitors to enjoy.
6. Nightlife and Entertainment: Koh Samet has a vibrant nightlife scene, especially around the main beaches. You can find beach bars, clubs, and restaurants offering live music, DJs, fire shows, and beach parties. Enjoy a cocktail, dance the night away, or simply relax and soak up the lively atmosphere.
7. Thai Massage and Wellness: Treat yourself to a traditional Thai massage or indulge in a wellness experience. There are numerous massage parlors and spas on the island where you can enjoy a rejuvenating massage, reflexology, or other therapeutic treatments.
8. Seafood Dining: Koh Samet is renowned for its fresh seafood. Visit one of the beachfront restaurants or seafood markets and savor a delicious seafood feast. Try local specialties like grilled prawns, spicy seafood soup, or fried fish with chili and garlic.

These are just a few of the activities and attractions available on Koh Samet. Whether you prefer relaxation, adventure, or exploration, the island offers something for everyone to enjoy.

Water Sports and Diving

Koh Samet offers a variety of water sports and diving activities for visitors to enjoy. Here are some popular options:

1. Snorkeling: Snorkeling is a great way to explore the vibrant underwater world surrounding Koh Samet. Rent snorkeling gear and head to one of the snorkeling spots, such as Ao Phai or Ao Nuan Beach, where you can observe colorful coral reefs and tropical fish. You can also join snorkeling tours that take you to multiple snorkeling sites around the island.
2. Diving: Koh Samet is home to several diving centers that offer diving courses and guided dives for all levels of experience. Discover the rich marine life and explore underwater caves, pinnacles, and coral gardens. Popular dive sites

around Koh Samet include Hin Khao, Koh Talu, and Koh Kudi. Whether you're a beginner or an experienced diver, there are diving options available to suit your skill level.
3. Jet Skiing: Experience the thrill of riding a jet ski along the pristine coastline of Koh Samet. Jet ski rentals are available at various beaches, allowing you to speed through the waters and enjoy the adrenaline rush. Please ensure that you follow safety guidelines and regulations while participating in jet skiing activities.
4. Kayaking: Rent a kayak and paddle along the calm waters surrounding Koh Samet. It's a peaceful and enjoyable way to explore the coastline, visit hidden coves, and discover secluded beaches. Kayaking allows you to go at your own pace and appreciate the natural beauty of the island from a different perspective.
5. Paddleboarding: Stand-up paddleboarding (SUP) has gained popularity in recent years, and Koh Samet offers the perfect setting for this activity. Rent a paddleboard and glide along the tranquil waters while enjoying views of the island's coastline. SUP is a great way to improve balance, get a workout, and connect with the beautiful surroundings.
6. Banana Boat Rides: For some family fun or group excitement, try a banana boat ride. Hold on

tight as you and your companions ride a banana-shaped inflatable boat pulled by a speedboat. It's a thrilling and enjoyable activity that guarantees laughter and excitement.

When participating in water sports and diving activities, it's essential to prioritize safety. Follow instructions from trained professionals, wear appropriate safety equipment, and be aware of your surroundings. Consider booking activities through reputable operators to ensure a safe and enjoyable experience.

Please note that availability of water sports and diving activities may vary depending on weather conditions and the time of year. It's always a good idea to check with local providers for up-to-date information and make reservations in advance, especially during peak tourist seasons.

Snorkeling Spots

Koh Samet offers several fantastic snorkeling spots where you can explore the underwater world and discover colorful marine life. Here are some popular snorkeling spots on the island:

1. Ao Phai: Located on the eastern side of Koh Samet, Ao Phai is known for its clear waters and vibrant coral reefs. Snorkelers can swim close to the shore and witness a variety of fish species, including butterflyfish, parrotfish, and angelfish. The rocky areas at the northern end of the beach are particularly good for snorkeling.
2. Ao Nuan: Ao Nuan Beach, situated on the southern tip of Koh Samet, is a secluded and tranquil spot with excellent snorkeling opportunities. The waters here are teeming with marine life, including colorful corals, clownfish, and damselfish. Snorkelers can explore the underwater world just a short distance from the beach.
3. Ao Wai: Ao Wai Beach is another recommended snorkeling spot on Koh Samet. The waters around Ao Wai are home to diverse marine life and coral formations. Snorkelers can encounter

schools of fish, sea anemones, and other fascinating underwater creatures. The beach's peaceful atmosphere also adds to the snorkeling experience.

4. Koh Talu: While not directly on Koh Samet, Koh Talu is a nearby island known for its excellent snorkeling opportunities. Located about an hour's boat ride from Koh Samet, Koh Talu offers pristine waters, beautiful coral reefs, and an abundance of marine life. Snorkelers can explore the underwater world around the island and discover an array of colorful fish and coral species.

5. Koh Kudi: Another popular snorkeling spot near Koh Samet is Koh Kudi. This small island is known for its crystal-clear waters and diverse marine ecosystem. Snorkelers can encounter various fish species, including angelfish, sergeant majors, and wrasses. The coral reefs around Koh Kudi are also home to interesting coral formations and sea anemones.

When snorkeling, it's important to follow responsible snorkeling practices, such as not touching or damaging the coral reefs, respecting marine life, and using reef-safe sunscreen to minimize environmental impact.

Consider renting snorkeling gear from reputable operators on the island or joining snorkeling tours that provide equipment and knowledgeable guides.

Please note that weather and sea conditions can affect snorkeling visibility and safety. It's advisable to check local weather forecasts and consult with tour operators or local experts for the most up-to-date information on snorkeling conditions during your visit to Koh Samet.

Hiking and Nature Trails

While Koh Samet is more known for its beaches and water activities, there are still opportunities for hiking and nature trails on the island. Here are some options for hiking and exploring nature on Koh Samet:

1. Khao Laem Ya - Mu Ko Samet National Park: Koh Samet is home to this national park, which covers both land and sea areas. Within the park, you'll find nature trails that allow you to explore the island's natural beauty and observe wildlife. One popular trail is the Khao Laem Ya Viewpoint Trail, which leads to the highest point on the island and offers panoramic views of the surrounding islands and coastline.
2. Ao Wong Duean Nature Trail: Located near Ao Wong Duean Beach, this nature trail takes you through a lush forested area. It's a relatively short and easy trail, perfect for a leisurely stroll. Along the way, you can enjoy the serene atmosphere, spot various plant species, and perhaps encounter some wildlife.
3. Ao Phrao Nature Trail: This trail starts from Ao Phrao Beach and meanders through the island's interior, offering a glimpse into the island's diverse flora and fauna. As you walk through the forested trail, you may encounter interesting plant species, butterflies, and occasional wildlife.
4. Beach-to-Beach Walks: While not traditional hiking trails, you can embark on beach-to-beach walks to explore different parts of the island. Walk along the coastline from one beach to another, enjoying the scenic views and discovering hidden spots along the way. For

example, you can walk from Sai Kaew Beach to Ao Phai Beach or from Ao Nuan Beach to Ao Wai Beach.

It's important to note that the hiking and nature trail options on Koh Samet are relatively limited compared to some other destinations. The island's main attractions are its beaches and marine activities. However, if you're interested in nature walks and exploring the island's natural surroundings, the options mentioned above can provide a glimpse into Koh Samet's inland beauty.

Remember to wear appropriate footwear, carry water, and respect the natural environment while hiking or walking on the trails.

Sunset Viewpoints

Koh Samet offers several stunning sunset viewpoints where you can enjoy the breathtaking beauty of the sun setting over the horizon. Here are some recommended spots for watching sunsets on the island:

1. Sai Kaew Beach: Sai Kaew Beach, also known as Diamond Beach, is one of the most popular and vibrant beaches on Koh Samet. The long stretch of sandy shoreline and its western-facing direction make it an ideal spot to witness magical sunsets. Grab a beach chair or find a cozy spot on the sand, and watch as the sky transforms into a palette of vibrant colors.
2. Ao Prao Beach: Located on the west coast of Koh Samet, Ao Prao Beach offers a serene and romantic setting for sunset viewing. The tranquil atmosphere and beautiful panoramic views make it a favorite spot for couples and those seeking a peaceful sunset experience. Relax on the beach, enjoy a refreshing drink, and witness the sun dipping below the horizon.
3. Ao Wong Duean Beach: With its picturesque setting and calm waters, Ao Wong Duean Beach is another fantastic spot to catch the sunset. As the sun lowers in the sky, you can sit back and soak up the peaceful ambiance while watching the colors change and reflect on the water. The laid-back beachfront restaurants and bars provide a comfortable vantage point to enjoy the view.

4. Viewpoints in Khao Laem Ya - Mu Ko Samet National Park: The national park on Koh Samet offers elevated viewpoints that provide stunning vistas of the surrounding islands and coastline. One of the popular viewpoints is the Khao Laem Ya Viewpoint, located on the highest point of the island. From here, you can witness panoramic views of the sea, beaches, and the setting sun.
5. Sunset Cruises: Consider taking a sunset cruise around Koh Samet to witness the sun setting from the sea. Several tour operators offer boat trips during the evening, allowing you to enjoy the changing colors of the sky while cruising along the coastline. It's a memorable way to experience the beauty of the sunset from a different perspective.

Remember to check the local sunset time and plan to arrive a bit earlier to secure a good spot. The exact views and colors of the sunset can vary depending on weather conditions and the time of year, so each sunset experience can be unique. Capture the moments with your camera or simply relax and take in the natural beauty unfolding before your eyes.

Boat Tours and Island Hopping

Koh Samet is surrounded by a cluster of picturesque islands and islets, making it an excellent destination for boat tours and island hopping. Here's a guide to boat tours and island hopping options in the Koh Samet area:

1. Island Hopping Tours: Many tour operators on Koh Samet offer island hopping tours that allow you to visit multiple islands in a single trip. These tours typically include stops at popular nearby islands such as Koh Kudi, Koh Talu, and Koh Thalu. You can explore their pristine beaches, snorkel in clear waters, and soak up the beauty of these secluded paradises.
2. Private Boat Charters: For a more personalized experience, you can arrange a private boat charter. Chartering a boat allows you to tailor your itinerary and explore the islands at your own pace. You can work with the boat operator to

create a customized island hopping experience that suits your preferences and interests.
3. Sunset Cruises: Enjoy the beauty of a Koh Samet sunset from the comfort of a boat. Sunset cruises are a popular option for a relaxing and romantic experience. Cruise along the coastline, watch the sun dip below the horizon, and witness the sky transforming into a vibrant canvas of colors. Some sunset cruises may include dinner or drinks on board to enhance the experience.
4. Fishing Tours: If you're a fishing enthusiast, consider joining a fishing tour around Koh Samet. These tours allow you to try your hand at fishing in the Gulf of Thailand. Whether you're a beginner or an experienced angler, you can enjoy the thrill of catching various fish species while enjoying the scenic views of the surrounding islands.
5. Snorkeling and Diving Excursions: Many boat tours in Koh Samet offer snorkeling and diving excursions to explore the underwater beauty of the surrounding islands. These tours take you to prime snorkeling and diving spots where you can immerse yourself in vibrant coral reefs, encounter colorful marine life, and discover the hidden treasures of the sea.

When booking boat tours or island hopping trips, it's important to choose reputable operators who prioritize safety and sustainability. They should provide well-maintained boats, experienced guides, and adhere to responsible tourism practices to minimize environmental impact.

Please note that availability and specific tour offerings may vary depending on the time of year and weather conditions. It's recommended to inquire with local tour operators or travel agencies on Koh Samet for up-to-date information and to make reservations in advance to secure your preferred tour.

Dining and Nightlife

Koh Samet offers a range of dining options and a vibrant nightlife scene that caters to different tastes and preferences. Here's a glimpse into the dining and nightlife experiences you can enjoy on the island:

Dining:

1. Beachfront Restaurants: Many of the beaches on Koh Samet are lined with beachfront restaurants and bars. These establishments offer a relaxed and casual atmosphere where you can enjoy a variety of Thai and international cuisines while taking in the beautiful views of the sea. Fresh seafood is often a highlight, with dishes such as grilled fish, prawns, and squid being popular choices.
2. Thai Street Food: Explore the streets of Koh Samet, particularly around the main villages and markets, to discover a wide array of delicious Thai street food. You can indulge in local favorites such as pad Thai, green curry, mango sticky rice, and various grilled skewers. These affordable and flavorful options allow you to sample authentic Thai flavors.
3. International Cuisine: In addition to Thai food, Koh Samet also offers a diverse range of international cuisines. You can find restaurants serving Western, Italian, Japanese, and other international dishes. Whether you're craving

pizza, pasta, sushi, or burgers, you'll find options to satisfy your taste buds.

Nightlife:

1. Beach Bars and Clubs: Koh Samet's beaches come alive after sunset with vibrant beach bars and clubs offering a lively nightlife experience. Enjoy refreshing cocktails, live music, and dance to the beats of DJs as you revel in the beachside atmosphere. Beach parties are also common, particularly during peak tourist seasons.
2. Fire Shows: Some beach bars and restaurants organize fire shows, where skilled performers showcase their fire-twirling and fire-dancing skills. These mesmerizing performances create an enchanting and thrilling ambiance as you watch the flames dance against the night sky.
3. Walking Street: Located near Sai Kaew Beach, the main village of Koh Samet, you'll find a bustling Walking Street area. This vibrant street is lined with shops, bars, and restaurants. You can wander through the bustling night market, shop for souvenirs, and enjoy the lively atmosphere.
4. Rooftop Bars: If you're looking for a more relaxed and upscale setting, consider visiting one of the rooftop bars on Koh Samet. These establishments offer panoramic views of the

island and the sea, making them ideal for enjoying a sunset drink or a nightcap under the stars.

It's worth noting that while Koh Samet offers a lively nightlife scene, it is relatively more relaxed compared to some other popular Thai destinations like Phuket or Pattaya. The island strikes a balance between offering vibrant nightlife options and maintaining its laid-back island charm.

Please be mindful of local regulations and respect the island's natural surroundings and communities while enjoying the dining and nightlife scene on Koh Samet.

Local Cuisine and Street Food

Koh Samet offers a delightful array of local cuisine and street food that allows you to indulge in authentic Thai flavors. Here are some popular dishes and street food options you can explore on the island:

1. Pad Thai: Pad Thai is a classic Thai dish that is widely enjoyed both locally and internationally. It consists of stir-fried rice noodles with tofu, shrimp or chicken, bean sprouts, eggs, and a tangy tamarind sauce. This flavorful and satisfying dish is a must-try when visiting Koh Samet.
2. Green Curry: Green curry is a fragrant and spicy Thai curry made with green chili paste, coconut milk, and a variety of vegetables and meats. It is typically served with steamed rice and offers a delightful combination of flavors and aromas.
3. Tom Yum Goong: Tom Yum Goong is a popular Thai soup known for its spicy and sour flavors. It is made with a fragrant broth infused with lemongrass, kaffir lime leaves, galangal, and chili. The soup is usually filled with succulent shrimp, mushrooms, and other herbs and spices.
4. Som Tam (Papaya Salad): Som Tam is a refreshing and spicy Thai salad made from shredded unripe papaya, tomatoes, carrots, green beans, peanuts, and a zesty dressing. It combines the flavors of sweet, sour, and spicy, creating a tantalizing culinary experience.
5. Grilled Seafood: Koh Samet is renowned for its fresh seafood offerings. You can savor a variety of grilled seafood, such as fish, prawns, squid, and scallops, cooked to perfection over charcoal

grills. The seafood is often served with spicy dipping sauces, steamed rice, and fresh vegetables.
6. Mango Sticky Rice: A popular Thai dessert, Mango Sticky Rice combines the sweetness of ripe mangoes with sticky glutinous rice, topped with a drizzle of coconut cream. It's a delightful and indulgent treat that perfectly balances flavors and textures.
7. Thai Street Food: Exploring the streets of Koh Samet will lead you to various street food stalls offering an array of delectable treats. You can find items like grilled skewers (known as "satay"), crispy spring rolls, fried chicken, spicy salads, and sweet snacks like banana pancakes and coconut pancakes.

As you wander through the main village of Koh Samet or the night markets, you'll have plenty of opportunities to sample the local street food. The island's street food scene offers an authentic and affordable way to experience Thai cuisine.

Don't hesitate to try new dishes and flavors, and feel free to ask locals for their recommendations. They can provide insights into their favorite local eateries and hidden gems that may not be as well-known to tourists. Enjoy the diverse flavors of Koh Samet's cuisine and savor the rich culinary traditions of Thailand.

Popular Restaurants and Cafes

Koh Samet offers a variety of popular restaurants and cafes where you can enjoy delicious meals, refreshing drinks, and a pleasant dining experience. Here are some notable options:

1. Tubtim Resort Restaurant: Located on Tubtim Beach, this beachfront restaurant offers a relaxed atmosphere and stunning views of the sea. It serves a range of Thai and international dishes, including fresh seafood, grilled meats, and vegetarian options.

2. Ploy Talay Restaurant: Situated on Ao Phai Beach, Ploy Talay Restaurant is known for its extensive seafood menu. You can choose from a variety of grilled fish, prawns, crabs, and shellfish. The restaurant offers a beachside dining experience with a lively atmosphere.
3. Chili Thai Restaurant: Found near Sai Kaew Beach, Chili Thai Restaurant is a popular spot for traditional Thai cuisine. From curries and stir-fries to soups and salads, the menu features a wide range of authentic Thai dishes prepared with fresh ingredients.
4. Samed Villa Resort Restaurant: This beachfront restaurant at Samed Villa Resort offers a serene setting and a diverse menu. You can enjoy both Thai and international dishes, along with fresh seafood and vegetarian options. The restaurant's terrace seating provides a picturesque view of the ocean.
5. Bueng Restaurant: Situated in the main village of Koh Samet, Bueng Restaurant is a cozy eatery that specializes in Thai cuisine. It offers a range of flavorful dishes, including stir-fries, curries, and traditional Thai soups. The restaurant has both indoor and outdoor seating options.
6. Drunken Sailors Coffee Bar: For coffee lovers, Drunken Sailors Coffee Bar is a popular choice. Located near Sai Kaew Beach, this cozy café

serves a variety of coffee beverages, teas, and light snacks. It's a great spot to relax and enjoy a cup of coffee in a laid-back atmosphere.
7. Naga Bar: Naga Bar is a beachfront bar and restaurant on Sai Kaew Beach known for its vibrant ambiance and live music. Apart from refreshing drinks, the menu offers a range of international dishes, including burgers, pizzas, and salads.

These are just a few examples of popular restaurants and cafes on Koh Samet. The island offers a wide range of dining options to suit different tastes and preferences. Whether you're looking for a beachfront dining experience, authentic Thai cuisine, or international flavors, Koh Samet has something to satisfy your cravings.

It's always a good idea to check the operating hours and make reservations, especially during peak tourist seasons, to ensure you secure a table at your preferred restaurant or café.

Nightlife and Entertainment Options

While Koh Samet may not have a wild and bustling nightlife scene like some other Thai destinations, it still offers a range of entertainment options to enjoy after the sun sets. Here are some popular nightlife and entertainment options on the island:

1. Beach Bars and Clubs: Koh Samet's beaches come alive at night with beach bars and clubs offering a lively atmosphere. You can enjoy refreshing cocktails, listen to live music, and dance the night away on the sandy shores. Some popular beach bars and clubs include Maya Bar, Silver Sand Bar, and 99 Rest Bar.
2. Fire Shows: Many beachfront establishments on Koh Samet organize fire shows, where skilled performers showcase their fire-twirling and

fire-dancing skills. These captivating shows create a mesmerizing ambiance as you watch the flames dance against the night sky.

3. Walking Street: Located near Sai Kaew Beach, the main village of Koh Samet, you'll find a bustling Walking Street area. This vibrant street is lined with shops, bars, restaurants, and small clubs. You can explore the night market, shop for souvenirs, and enjoy the lively atmosphere.

4. Live Music Venues: Several bars and restaurants on Koh Samet feature live music performances, adding to the island's nightlife charm. You can find local bands and musicians playing a variety of genres, including Thai music, classic hits, and contemporary tunes.

5. Sunset Cruises: Take a sunset cruise around Koh Samet for a relaxing and romantic experience. You can enjoy the changing colors of the sky while cruising along the coastline. Some sunset cruises may include dinner or drinks on board, enhancing the experience.

6. Quiet Beach Walks: If you prefer a more relaxed and peaceful evening, take a stroll along the quiet beaches of Koh Samet under the moonlight. Enjoy the soothing sound of the waves and the gentle breeze as you take in the serene atmosphere.

It's important to note that Koh Samet's nightlife is relatively more laid-back and relaxed compared to some other Thai party destinations. The island strikes a balance between offering entertainment options and maintaining its tranquil island charm. It's always a good idea to check with locals or fellow travelers for recommendations on the current nightlife scene and any special events happening during your visit.

As with any nightlife experience, it's essential to drink responsibly, respect the local culture and environment, and be aware of your personal safety

Accommodation Options

Koh Samet offers a range of accommodation options to suit different preferences and budgets. Whether you're looking for beachfront resorts, budget-friendly guesthouses, or cozy bungalows, you'll find a variety of choices on the island. Here are some popular accommodation options on Koh Samet:

1. Beachfront Resorts: Koh Samet is known for its beautiful beachfront resorts that offer stunning ocean views, direct beach access, and a range of amenities. These resorts often feature spacious rooms or villas, swimming pools, on-site restaurants, bars, and spa facilities. Some popular beachfront resorts include Sai Kaew Beach Resort, Paradee Resort, and Le Vimarn Cottages & Spa.
2. Budget Guesthouses: If you're looking for more affordable options, Koh Samet has a number of budget guesthouses and hostels. These accommodations typically offer basic rooms or dormitory-style beds with shared facilities. They provide a comfortable and budget-friendly option for travelers who are more focused on exploring the island than spending time in luxurious accommodations.
3. Bungalows: Koh Samet is also known for its charming beach bungalows. These standalone units are often nestled amidst lush tropical

gardens and provide a cozy and rustic ambiance. Bungalows offer a more intimate and secluded accommodation experience, with options ranging from basic to more upscale bungalow resorts.
4. Boutique Hotels: If you're looking for a unique and stylish accommodation experience, consider staying in one of Koh Samet's boutique hotels. These establishments often feature individually designed rooms with personalized touches, creating a more intimate and exclusive atmosphere.
5. Mid-Range Hotels: Koh Samet offers a variety of mid-range hotels that strike a balance between comfort and affordability. These hotels typically provide comfortable rooms, on-site dining options, and sometimes swimming pools or spa facilities.

When choosing accommodation on Koh Samet, it's important to consider factors such as location, amenities, and proximity to the beach or other attractions. It's also advisable to book in advance, especially during peak seasons, to secure your preferred accommodation.

Whether you're seeking a luxurious beachfront retreat or a cozy budget-friendly stay, Koh Samet has options to cater to various preferences and budgets. It's recommended to read reviews, compare prices, and choose an accommodation that best fits your needs for a memorable stay on the island.

Resorts and Hotel

Koh Samet offers a variety of resorts and hotels to cater to different tastes and budgets. Here are some popular resorts and hotels on the island:

1. Sai Kaew Beach Resort: Located on Sai Kaew Beach, Sai Kaew Beach Resort is a well-known and popular beachfront resort. It offers a range of accommodation options, from standard rooms to luxurious villas. The resort features multiple

swimming pools, beachfront dining options, a spa, and various recreational activities.
2. Paradee Resort: Paradee Resort is a luxurious beachfront resort nestled on Ao Kiew Beach. It offers spacious villas with private pools, stunning ocean views, and direct beach access. The resort provides a tranquil and upscale atmosphere, perfect for a relaxing getaway.
3. Le Vimarn Cottages & Spa: Situated on Ao Prao Beach, Le Vimarn Cottages & Spa is a boutique resort known for its unique cottages designed in traditional Thai style. The resort features a spa, a beachfront restaurant, and beautiful views of the sea.
4. Mooban Talay Resort: Mooban Talay Resort offers cozy and comfortable bungalows nestled in a peaceful garden setting. Located near Sai Kaew Beach, the resort provides a quiet retreat while still being within walking distance of the beach and village.
5. Lima Coco Resort: Lima Coco Resort is a beachfront resort on Ao Phai Beach. It offers modern rooms and villas with private balconies or terraces. The resort features a swimming pool, beachfront dining options, and a bar.
6. Pandora Resort: Pandora Resort is a mid-range beachfront resort on Ao Phai Beach. It offers comfortable rooms with modern amenities and

beach views. The resort has a swimming pool, a beachside restaurant, and a bar.
7. Tubtim Resort: Tubtim Resort is a cozy beachfront resort located on Tubtim Beach. It offers bungalows and rooms with ocean views and direct beach access. The resort features a restaurant and a beach bar.

When choosing a resort or hotel on Koh Samet, consider factors such as location, amenities, room types, and pricing. It's recommended to check reviews and compare prices to find the accommodation that best suits your preferences and budget.

Please note that the availability and offerings of resorts and hotels may vary, so it's advisable to check their websites or contact them directly for the most up-to-date information and to make reservations in advance, especially during peak travel seasons.

Budget and Backpacker Accommodations

If you're a budget traveler or backpacker, Koh Samet offers a range of affordable accommodation options that provide comfortable stays without breaking the bank. Here are some budget and backpacker accommodations on the island:

1. Samed Villa Resort: Samed Villa Resort offers both budget-friendly rooms and bungalows. The resort is located near Sai Kaew Beach and provides easy access to the main village area.
2. Silver Sand Pub & Restaurant: Situated on Sai Kaew Beach, Silver Sand Pub & Restaurant offers budget-friendly rooms and dormitory-style accommodations. It's a popular choice among backpackers due to its central location and lively atmosphere.
3. Nimmanoradee Resort: Nimmanoradee Resort offers budget-friendly bungalows and rooms on Ao Kiew Beach. The resort provides a peaceful and laid-back atmosphere away from the main tourist areas.

4. Tubtim Resort: Tubtim Resort offers budget-friendly accommodation options including bungalows and rooms. It is located on Tubtim Beach, providing a serene setting and a more relaxed atmosphere.
5. Ban Rak Samed: Ban Rak Samed is a guesthouse located near Sai Kaew Beach. It offers budget-friendly rooms with basic amenities and a convenient location close to the beach and main village area.
6. Runa Runa The Best Guesthouse: Situated near Sai Kaew Beach, Runa Runa The Best Guesthouse offers affordable rooms with basic facilities. It provides a cozy and friendly atmosphere for budget-conscious travelers.
7. Lima Bella Resort: Lima Bella Resort offers budget-friendly rooms and bungalows near Ao Phai Beach. It provides a comfortable stay at an affordable price point.

When booking budget and backpacker accommodations, it's important to consider the location, facilities, and reviews from other travelers. While these options may offer more basic amenities compared to higher-end resorts, they provide a cost-effective way to enjoy your stay on Koh Samet.

It's advisable to make reservations in advance, especially during peak seasons, to secure your preferred accommodation. Additionally, keep in mind that the availability and offerings of budget accommodations may vary, so it's recommended to check their websites or contact them directly for the most up-to-date information.

Beachfront Bungalows

Koh Samet is known for its beachfront bungalows, which offer a rustic and idyllic accommodation experience right by the sea. Here are some beachfront bungalow options on the island:

1. Ao Prao Resort: Ao Prao Resort is located on Ao Prao Beach and offers beachfront bungalows with stunning ocean views. The bungalows are

well-appointed and provide a peaceful and private retreat.
2. Ao Cho Grand View Resort: Situated on Ao Cho Beach, Ao Cho Grand View Resort offers beachfront bungalows with direct access to the beach. The bungalows are equipped with modern amenities and feature private balconies or terraces.
3. Mooban Talay Resort: Mooban Talay Resort offers beachfront bungalows nestled in a tranquil garden setting near Sai Kaew Beach. The bungalows provide a cozy and peaceful stay, with easy access to the beach and nearby attractions.
4. Tubtim Resort: Tubtim Resort is located on Tubtim Beach and offers beachfront bungalows with beautiful sea views. The bungalows are simple yet comfortable, providing an authentic beachfront experience.
5. Lima Coco Resort: Lima Coco Resort is situated on Ao Phai Beach and offers beachfront bungalows with direct beach access. The bungalows are well-designed and provide a comfortable stay by the sea.
6. Nimmanoradee Resort: Nimmanoradee Resort offers beachfront bungalows on Ao Kiew Beach. The bungalows are set amidst a peaceful environment and offer a serene getaway right on the beach.

These are just a few examples of beachfront bungalow accommodations on Koh Samet. Each resort or property may have its own unique style and amenities, so it's recommended to research and compare options based on your preferences.

When booking beachfront bungalows, it's advisable to check the facilities provided, such as private bathrooms, air conditioning, and in-room amenities. Additionally, consider the location and proximity to other attractions or dining options.

As beachfront bungalows are often in high demand, it's recommended to make reservations in advance, especially during peak travel seasons, to secure your preferred accommodation.

Local Culture and Festivals

Koh Samet, like many other places in Thailand, has a rich local culture and celebrates various festivals throughout the year. Here are some of the significant cultural aspects and festivals you can experience on the island:

1. Thai Buddhist Culture: Buddhism plays a significant role in Thai culture, and you can observe the influence of Buddhism on Koh Samet. You may come across Buddhist temples (called "wat") where locals and visitors can make offerings and participate in religious ceremonies.
2. Loy Krathong: Loy Krathong is a popular Thai festival celebrated nationwide, usually in November. During this festival, people release small decorated floats (krathongs) onto water bodies as a symbolic gesture to let go of negative

energy and start anew. On Koh Samet, you may find special events or celebrations organized by resorts or local communities.
3. Songkran: Songkran is the traditional Thai New Year celebrated from April 13th to 15th each year. It is a lively and joyous festival where people participate in water fights and perform traditional rituals to mark the arrival of the new year. Koh Samet also joins in the festivities, with locals and visitors engaging in water splashing activities and enjoying cultural performances.
4. Thai Food Culture: Thailand is renowned for its delicious cuisine, and Koh Samet offers a chance to indulge in traditional Thai dishes. You can explore local food markets, street vendors, and restaurants to savor authentic Thai flavors, including spicy curries, fresh seafood, and aromatic stir-fried dishes.
5. Muay Thai: Muay Thai, also known as Thai kickboxing, is the national sport of Thailand and deeply ingrained in Thai culture. On Koh Samet, you may have the opportunity to watch Muay Thai fights or even participate in training sessions at local gyms.

It's worth noting that while these cultural aspects are present on Koh Samet, the island is primarily known for its beach and natural attractions. To experience a broader range of cultural festivals and activities, you may want to consider visiting mainland Thailand or larger cities that offer a more diverse cultural scene.

When participating in cultural events or visiting religious sites, it's important to respect local customs, dress modestly, and follow any guidelines or rules set by the authorities or organizers. This shows appreciation for the local culture and ensures a positive experience for everyone involved.

Traditional Thai Customs

Thailand has a rich cultural heritage with a set of traditional customs and etiquette that are observed and valued by the Thai people. When visiting Thailand, including Koh Samet, it's helpful to be aware of these customs and practice them to show respect for the local culture. Here are some traditional Thai customs to keep in mind:

1. Wai Greeting: The traditional Thai greeting is known as the "wai." It involves placing your palms together in a prayer-like gesture and slightly bowing your head. Thais use the wai to greet others, show respect, and express gratitude. When interacting with locals, it's appropriate to return the wai gesture.
2. Modest Dress: In Thai culture, modesty in dress is valued, especially when visiting temples or sacred sites. It's advisable to dress modestly by covering your shoulders, avoiding revealing clothing, and wearing long pants or skirts when visiting religious places. Respectful attire is also appreciated in other public areas, although beachwear is acceptable on the beaches.

3. Removing Shoes: It's customary to remove your shoes before entering temples, private homes, and some shops or establishments. Look for cues, such as a pile of shoes at the entrance, to determine if shoe removal is required. Keeping your feet clean and avoiding pointing your feet directly at people or sacred objects is also considered polite.
4. Respecting Monks: Thailand is a predominantly Buddhist country, and monks hold a revered position in society. When encountering a monk, it's respectful to give them space and avoid physical contact. Women should avoid touching or handing objects directly to monks, as they follow certain guidelines regarding gender interactions.
5. Polite Behavior: Thais value politeness and maintaining a harmonious atmosphere. It's advisable to use polite language, smile, and be patient in your interactions. Public displays of anger or impatience are generally frowned upon.
6. Food Etiquette: When dining with Thais, it's customary to wait for the host or senior person to start eating before you begin. When sharing dishes, use serving spoons or separate utensils to take food onto your plate. It's also polite to try a bit of everything offered to you as a sign of appreciation.

7. Royal Respect: The Thai monarchy is highly revered, and it's essential to show respect towards the royal family. Criticizing or making disrespectful comments about the monarchy is not only impolite but also illegal.

By observing these traditional customs, you can show respect for Thai culture and create positive interactions with locals during your visit to Koh Samet or any other part of Thailand. Thais are generally understanding of cultural differences, but your efforts to embrace their customs will be appreciated.

Festivals and Celebrations

Koh Samet, like the rest of Thailand, celebrates several festivals and cultural events throughout the year. While the island may not host large-scale festivities, you can still experience the local charm and participate in some traditional celebrations. Here are a few festivals and celebrations that you may encounter on Koh Samet:

1. Songkran: Songkran is the Thai New Year festival, celebrated in mid-April. It is a water festival where people engage in playful water fights to symbolize the washing away of the previous year's misfortunes and welcoming the new year with a fresh start. On Koh Samet, you can expect water splashing activities and lively celebrations.
2. Loy Krathong: Loy Krathong usually falls in November and is a festival of lights. People release krathongs (decorated floats) into rivers, lakes, or the sea, accompanied by candlelight. It's a beautiful sight and symbolizes letting go of negative energy and making wishes for the future. You may find special events or ceremonies organized by resorts or local communities.
3. Buddhist Festivals: As a predominantly Buddhist country, Thailand celebrates several Buddhist festivals throughout the year. These include Makha Bucha, Visakha Bucha, and Asalha Bucha, which commemorate important events in the life of Buddha and involve merit-making

activities, temple visits, and candlelit processions. Local temples on Koh Samet may hold special ceremonies during these occasions.
4. Local Village Festivals: The villages on Koh Samet occasionally organize local festivals, often showcasing traditional Thai music, dance performances, and food stalls. These events provide an opportunity to experience the island's local culture, interact with locals, and savor delicious Thai cuisine.

It's important to note that festival dates may vary slightly each year, as they follow the Thai lunar calendar. It's advisable to check the specific dates and events closer to your travel dates or consult with the locals or your accommodation for any upcoming festivities during your visit.

Attending these festivals and celebrations can offer a glimpse into Thai traditions, cultural practices, and the warm hospitality of the locals. Embrace the festive spirit, participate respectfully, and immerse yourself in the vibrant atmosphere to create memorable experiences on Koh Samet.

Practical Information

Certainly! Here is some practical information that can be useful for your visit to Koh Samet:

1. Currency: The official currency of Thailand is the Thai Baht (THB). Currency exchange services are available on the island, and ATMs can be found in the main village area. Credit cards are widely accepted in resorts, hotels, and larger establishments, but it's advisable to carry some cash for smaller local businesses.
2. Language: The official language is Thai. While English is spoken and understood to some extent in tourist areas, it's helpful to carry a phrasebook or use translation apps to communicate with locals.
3. Climate: Koh Samet has a tropical climate characterized by hot and humid weather throughout the year. The dry season generally lasts from November to April, with January to

March being the driest months. The rainy season occurs from May to October, with occasional showers and storms. Pack lightweight and breathable clothing, sunscreen, a hat, and insect repellent.
4. Electricity: The standard electrical voltage in Thailand is 220V, and the plugs are typically the two-pin flat or round types. It's advisable to carry a universal adapter if your electronic devices have different plug types.
5. Health and Safety: Koh Samet is generally a safe destination for travelers. However, it's always wise to take standard precautions such as securing your belongings, avoiding isolated areas at night, and using reliable transportation. Remember to stay hydrated, use sunscreen, and protect yourself against mosquito bites. It's also recommended to have travel insurance that covers medical expenses.
6. Transportation: Motorized vehicles are not permitted on the island, so most transportation is done on foot or by motorcycle taxis. You can also rent bicycles or explore the island on foot. Long-tail boats are available for traveling to and from the island. Songthaews (shared pick-up trucks) provide transportation from the mainland to the pier.

7. Wi-Fi and Mobile Connectivity: Most resorts, hotels, and cafes on Koh Samet offer Wi-Fi access for guests. You can also purchase a local SIM card at the pier or in the main village area for mobile data.
8. National Park Fee: Koh Samet is part of the Khao Laem Ya-Mu Ko Samet National Park, and there is an entrance fee for visitors. As of my knowledge cutoff in September 2021, the fee for foreigners was around 200 THB per person. Please note that fees and regulations may change, so it's best to inquire about the current rates at the park entrance.

Remember to check the latest travel advisories and guidelines from your government regarding travel to Thailand and any specific requirements for entry or COVID-19 protocols.

With these practical details in mind, you'll be well-prepared to enjoy your visit to Koh Samet and have a memorable experience on the island.

Weather and Best Time to Visit

The weather in Koh Samet is characterized by a tropical climate with high temperatures and humidity throughout the year. The best time to visit depends on your preferences and the activities you plan to engage in. Here's an overview of the weather conditions and the recommended time to visit Koh Samet:

1. Dry Season (November to April): This period is considered the peak tourist season in Koh Samet due to the relatively low rainfall and pleasant weather. The months of December to February are particularly popular, offering cooler temperatures and less humidity. It's an ideal time for beach activities, sunbathing, snorkeling, and diving. However, keep in mind that this is also the busiest time, and accommodation prices may be higher. Advance bookings are recommended.
2. Rainy Season (May to October): The rainy season in Koh Samet brings higher chances of rainfall, but it's not constant downpour

throughout the day. The rain showers are often short-lived, followed by sunny intervals. This period is considered the low season, offering fewer crowds and lower accommodation rates. If you don't mind occasional rain and prefer a quieter and more affordable experience, the rainy season can be a good time to visit. However, do note that some water activities and boat tours may be limited during this time.

It's important to note that weather patterns can vary, and climate change may impact typical weather patterns. It's always advisable to check the weather forecast before your trip and be prepared for any unexpected changes.

Overall, the months of November to April offer a more reliable and pleasant weather experience, making it the popular choice for many visitors. However, if you prefer fewer crowds and don't mind occasional rain showers, the rainy season can still provide an enjoyable experience on the island.

Regardless of the season, it's recommended to bring lightweight and breathable clothing, sunscreen, a hat, and insect repellent to protect yourself from the sun and insects. Keep in mind that the island can be busy during holidays and long weekends, both during the dry and rainy seasons, so plan accordingly.

Remember to check for any travel advisories or updates regarding weather conditions and be prepared for changes in your itinerary if necessary.

Money and Currency Exchange

The official currency of Thailand is the Thai Baht (THB). Here is some information about money and currency exchange in Koh Samet:

1. Currency Exchange: Currency exchange services are available on Koh Samet, particularly in the main village area near the pier. You can exchange major foreign currencies such as US dollars, Euros, British pounds, and others to Thai Baht. It's advisable to compare exchange rates and fees at different exchange booths to get the best rates.
2. ATMs: There are ATMs available on Koh Samet where you can withdraw Thai Baht using your debit or credit card. Most ATMs accept major international cards such as Visa and Mastercard. Keep in mind that some smaller businesses may only accept cash, so it's a good idea to have some cash on hand.
3. Credit Cards: Credit cards are widely accepted in larger establishments such as resorts, hotels, restaurants, and shops on Koh Samet. However, it's advisable to carry some cash for smaller local businesses, street vendors, and transportation options like motorcycle taxis.
4. Traveler's Checks: Traveler's checks are not commonly used in Thailand, and it may be challenging to find places that accept them on Koh Samet. It's better to rely on cash or card payments.
5. Currency Exchange Tips: When exchanging money or using ATMs, be aware of the exchange rates and any applicable fees or commissions.

Some exchange booths may have better rates than others, so it's worth comparing before making a transaction. Additionally, notify your bank or credit card provider about your travel plans to Thailand to ensure smooth transactions and avoid any issues with your cards.
6. Small Denominations: It's a good idea to have smaller denomination Thai Baht notes (20s, 50s, 100s) as they are more convenient for daily expenses, especially for purchasing street food, small items, or paying for local transportation.
7. Safety and Security: Exercise caution when handling money and be mindful of your surroundings. It's advisable to keep your cash, cards, and valuable belongings secure, preferably in a hotel safe or a hidden money belt/pouch.

It's important to note that exchange rates and fees can vary, so it's recommended to check the current rates and any applicable charges before making transactions. Also, be cautious of unauthorized money changers and ensure you are dealing with reputable and licensed exchange services.

By being prepared with Thai Baht currency or having access to ATMs and credit cards, you can easily manage your finances during your stay on Koh Samet.

Safety Tips

Koh Samet is generally a safe destination for travelers, but it's always important to prioritize your safety and well-being during your visit. Here are some safety tips to keep in mind:

1. Personal Belongings: Take care of your personal belongings and valuables, especially in crowded areas and tourist spots. Keep an eye on your belongings and avoid leaving them unattended. Use hotel safes or secure lockers to store your valuables when not in use.

2. Water Safety: While enjoying water activities, be cautious of strong currents and always follow safety guidelines provided by tour operators or lifeguards. If you're not a strong swimmer, consider wearing a life jacket during water activities. Stay within designated swimming areas and be mindful of changing weather conditions.
3. Transportation: If you're renting a motorcycle or scooter, make sure you have a valid license and wear a helmet. Follow traffic rules and be cautious on the roads. Use authorized taxi services or motorcycle taxis for transportation, and negotiate the fare in advance if using motorcycle taxis.
4. Health and Hygiene: Stay hydrated by drinking plenty of water, especially in the hot and humid climate. Use sunscreen to protect your skin from the sun's rays. Practice good hygiene by washing your hands regularly, particularly before eating.
5. Street Food: Thailand is renowned for its delicious street food. While enjoying street food, choose stalls that have a high turnover of customers to ensure freshness. Look for clean food preparation areas and make sure the food is cooked thoroughly.
6. Scams and Touts: Be cautious of scams and touts that may try to take advantage of tourists.

Exercise caution when approached by strangers offering unsolicited services or deals that seem too good to be true. Use reputable tour operators and be skeptical of overly cheap or suspicious offers.
7. Local Laws and Customs: Familiarize yourself with local laws and customs to avoid any inadvertent legal or cultural issues. Respect local customs, traditions, and religious sites. Avoid criticizing or disrespecting the Thai monarchy, as it is a serious offense in Thailand.
8. Emergency Services: Save important contact numbers such as the local police, hospital, and your embassy or consulate in case of emergencies. If you require medical assistance, seek help from reputable healthcare facilities or contact your accommodation for guidance.
9. Travel Insurance: It's highly recommended to have travel insurance that covers medical expenses, emergency evacuation, and personal belongings. Review your insurance policy to ensure it provides adequate coverage for your needs.

Remember to use common sense, trust your instincts, and exercise caution while exploring Koh Samet. By being mindful of your surroundings and following these safety tips, you can have a safe and enjoyable experience on the island.

Health and Medical Facilities

Koh Samet has medical facilities and services to cater to the healthcare needs of visitors. Here is some information about health and medical facilities on the island:

1. Medical Clinics: There are several medical clinics on Koh Samet that provide basic medical services and treatments for minor illnesses, injuries, and common ailments. These clinics are staffed by qualified doctors and nurses who can offer medical advice and administer treatments. However, it's important to note that the medical clinics on the island may have limited facilities compared to larger hospitals.
2. Pharmacies: There are pharmacies available on Koh Samet where you can purchase

over-the-counter medications, basic first aid supplies, and other health-related products. The staff at these pharmacies can assist you with common ailments and provide advice on medications. However, for more serious conditions or prescription medications, it's advisable to consult a doctor or visit a hospital.

3. Hospitals and Emergency Services: In case of serious medical emergencies or conditions requiring advanced medical care, the nearest major hospitals are located on the mainland in Rayong or Pattaya. These hospitals are equipped with comprehensive medical facilities and services. In case of an emergency, you can contact local authorities or your accommodation for assistance and guidance.

4. Travel Insurance: It's highly recommended to have travel insurance that includes coverage for medical expenses and emergency medical evacuation. Before traveling, review your insurance policy to ensure it provides adequate coverage for your needs. In case of any medical issues, contact your insurance provider for guidance and assistance.

It's important to note that communication with medical professionals on Koh Samet may be easier if you have a basic understanding of the local language or have access to translation services or apps. It's also advisable to carry a copy of your medical records, prescriptions, and any important medical information that may be relevant during your visit.

As with any travel destination, it's wise to take necessary precautions to maintain good health during your stay on Koh Samet. Stay hydrated, practice good hygiene, protect yourself from the sun, and avoid consuming tap water. If you have any pre-existing medical conditions, it's recommended to consult your healthcare provider before your trip.

By being prepared and aware of the available medical facilities and services, you can ensure your health and well-being while enjoying your time on Koh Samet.

Communication and Internet Access

Communication and internet access on Koh Samet are generally available, allowing you to stay connected during your visit. Here's some information about communication options on the island:

1. Mobile Network Coverage: Major mobile network operators in Thailand, such as AIS, TrueMove H, and dtac, provide coverage on Koh Samet. You can purchase a local SIM card at the pier or in the main village area to have access to mobile data, calls, and text messages. The availability and strength of the signal may vary in certain areas of the island.
2. Wi-Fi: Many resorts, hotels, restaurants, cafes, and public areas on Koh Samet offer Wi-Fi access for their guests. You can connect to the Wi-Fi network provided by your accommodation or visit cafes and restaurants that offer free Wi-Fi. The quality and speed of Wi-Fi may vary depending on the establishment.
3. Internet Cafes: There are internet cafes available on the island where you can use their computers

and internet connection for a fee. These internet cafes typically have stable internet access and can be an option if you don't have your own device.
4. Roaming: If you have an international mobile plan with roaming capabilities, you may be able to use your mobile data, calls, and text messages on Koh Samet. However, roaming charges can be expensive, so it's advisable to check with your service provider about applicable rates and data limits before using roaming services.
5. Communication Apps: Popular communication apps such as WhatsApp, Line, and Skype are widely used in Thailand. If you have access to Wi-Fi or mobile data, you can use these apps to make calls, send messages, and video chat with friends and family.

Remember to check with your mobile service provider about international roaming charges and data packages that may be available specifically for Thailand. Also, be mindful of your data usage if you're relying on mobile data, as excessive usage may lead to additional charges or reduced internet speed.

By having access to mobile networks, Wi-Fi, or internet cafes, you can stay connected with loved ones, access information, and navigate your way around Koh Samet with ease.

Exploring Nearby Islands and Attractions

Koh Samet is located in the Gulf of Thailand and is surrounded by other beautiful islands and attractions that you can explore. Here are some nearby islands and attractions that you may consider visiting during your time in Koh Samet:

1. Koh Chang: Located to the south of Koh Samet, Koh Chang is the second-largest island in Thailand and offers stunning beaches, lush jungles, and waterfalls. You can enjoy activities such as snorkeling, diving, jungle trekking, and visiting local fishing villages.

2. Koh Kood: Koh Kood, also known as Koh Kut, is another picturesque island located near Koh Samet. It's known for its pristine beaches, clear turquoise waters, and tranquil atmosphere. You can relax on the beautiful beaches, explore waterfalls, and indulge in snorkeling or diving in the surrounding coral reefs.
3. Koh Mak: Koh Mak is a small island situated close to Koh Kood. It's known for its tranquil and laid-back atmosphere, making it a perfect escape for relaxation. You can explore its beautiful beaches, rent a bicycle to tour the island, and enjoy snorkeling or kayaking in the crystal-clear waters.
4. Rayong: Rayong is a province on the mainland near Koh Samet and offers a mix of natural beauty and cultural attractions. You can visit the Rayong Aquarium, explore the Khao Laem Ya - Mu Ko Samet National Park, or take a trip to the nearby Khao Chamao - Khao Wong National Park to experience the beauty of nature.
5. Ban Phe: Ban Phe is a small fishing village located on the mainland near Koh Samet. It's the departure point for boats heading to Koh Samet, but it also has its own charm. You can visit the local fish market, explore the village's laid-back atmosphere, and try fresh seafood in the local restaurants.

When planning a visit to these nearby islands and attractions, consider the transportation options available, such as ferry services or private boat tours. It's advisable to check the schedules and availability of transportation in advance, especially during peak seasons.

Exploring the nearby islands and attractions will give you a chance to experience the diversity and natural beauty of the Gulf of Thailand region, beyond the confines of Koh Samet.

Koh Chang

Koh Chang is a stunning island located in the Gulf of Thailand, known for its natural beauty, pristine beaches, lush rainforests, and waterfalls. Here's some information about Koh Chang that you may find helpful:

1. Beaches: Koh Chang is home to a variety of beautiful beaches, each offering its own charm. White Sand Beach (Hat Sai Khao) is the most popular and developed beach on the island, featuring a long stretch of white sandy beach lined with resorts, restaurants, and shops. Other notable beaches include Klong Prao Beach, Kai Bae Beach, Lonely Beach, and Bang Bao Beach.
2. Nature and Adventure: Koh Chang is renowned for its rich biodiversity and lush rainforests. Explore the island's interior by taking a jungle trek to discover hidden waterfalls such as Klong Plu Waterfall and Than Mayom Waterfall. Adventure seekers can engage in activities like zip-lining, elephant trekking, and kayaking through mangroves.
3. Snorkeling and Diving: The waters around Koh Chang are teeming with marine life, making it a great destination for snorkeling and diving. Koh Rang National Marine Park, located off the southwestern coast of the island, is known for its vibrant coral reefs and diverse marine ecosystem.
4. Island Hopping: Koh Chang serves as a hub for exploring nearby smaller islands. You can take a boat tour or hire a private boat to visit islands like Koh Wai, Koh Mak, and Koh Kham. These islands offer secluded beaches, crystal-clear waters, and a tranquil atmosphere.

5. Local Culture: Experience the local culture of Koh Chang by visiting fishing villages, exploring traditional temples, and indulging in authentic Thai cuisine. Bang Bao Village, built on stilts over the water, is a popular spot to observe local life, enjoy seafood restaurants, and go on fishing excursions.
6. Nightlife: While not as vibrant as some other Thai islands, Koh Chang does offer a selection of bars, beach clubs, and live music venues. The nightlife scene is concentrated mainly in the White Sand Beach and Lonely Beach areas.
7. Accommodation: Koh Chang offers a wide range of accommodation options to suit various budgets and preferences. You'll find luxury resorts, beachfront bungalows, mid-range hotels, and budget guesthouses scattered across the island.

To reach Koh Chang, you can take a ferry or speedboat from mainland ports like Laem Ngop or Ao Thammachat. The journey typically takes around 30 minutes to 1 hour, depending on the departure point and weather conditions.

Whether you're seeking relaxation on pristine beaches, adventure in the rainforest, or underwater exploration, Koh Chang offers a diverse range of experiences that make it a popular destination for travelers in Thailand.

Koh Kood

Koh Kood, also known as Koh Kut, is a picturesque and relatively undeveloped island located in the Gulf of Thailand, near the Cambodian border. Known for its pristine beaches, crystal-clear waters, and lush tropical forests, Koh Kood offers a tranquil and secluded getaway. Here's some information about Koh Kood that you may find useful:

1. Beaches: Koh Kood boasts some of Thailand's most stunning beaches. Sai Daeng Beach, located on the eastern coast, is known for its white sand and clear waters. Klong Chao Beach, on the western coast, offers a picturesque setting with palm trees and calm waters. Other beautiful beaches include Ao Phrao Beach, Khlong Hin Beach, and Bang Bao Beach.
2. Water Activities: Koh Kood is a paradise for water lovers. You can go swimming, snorkeling, and diving to explore the colorful coral reefs and vibrant marine life. Kayaking, paddleboarding, and boat tours are also popular activities to enjoy the island's natural beauty.
3. Waterfalls: The island is home to several enchanting waterfalls, including Klong Chao Waterfall and Huang Nam Keaw Waterfall. These cascades offer refreshing swimming spots and are surrounded by lush vegetation, making them perfect for nature lovers and adventurers.
4. Nature Trails: Koh Kood is blessed with lush rainforests and jungles, which are ideal for exploring on foot. Trekking trails take you through the island's dense vegetation, allowing you to discover hidden viewpoints, wildlife, and serene spots away from the beaches.
5. Island Hopping: Koh Kood serves as a base for exploring nearby islands, such as Koh Mak and

Koh Rayang. These islands offer similar natural beauty, tranquil beaches, and snorkeling opportunities, allowing you to create a unique island-hopping experience.
6. Local Village Life: Experience the local way of life by visiting fishing villages and interacting with the friendly locals. Take a stroll through the village of Ao Yai, where you can see traditional wooden houses, local shops, and enjoy fresh seafood in local restaurants.
7. Accommodation: Koh Kood offers a range of accommodation options, including beachfront resorts, bungalows, and eco-lodges. Many accommodations provide a peaceful and secluded atmosphere, allowing you to fully immerse yourself in the island's natural surroundings.

To reach Koh Kood, you can take a ferry or speedboat from the mainland ports of Laem Sok or Trat. The journey takes approximately 1.5 to 2 hours, depending on the departure point and sea conditions.

Koh Kood offers a serene and unspoiled island experience, making it an ideal destination for those seeking tranquility and natural beauty. Whether you want to relax on pristine beaches, explore the underwater world, or immerse yourself in lush greenery, Koh Kood is sure to leave you enchanted.

Rayong City

Rayong City is a vibrant and charming coastal city located on the eastern coast of Thailand. Situated approximately 179 kilometers southeast of Bangkok, Rayong City offers a mix of natural beauty, cultural attractions, and a bustling city atmosphere. Here's some information about Rayong City that you may find helpful:

1. Beaches: Rayong City is renowned for its beautiful beaches along the Gulf of Thailand. Mae Ramphueng Beach is one of the most popular beaches in the area, featuring a long stretch of golden sand and clear waters. Laem Mae Phim Beach is another picturesque spot with

calm and shallow waters, perfect for swimming and sunbathing.
2. Rayong Aquarium: Located near Mae Ramphueng Beach, Rayong Aquarium is a popular attraction for families and marine enthusiasts. The aquarium showcases various marine species found in the Gulf of Thailand, including colorful tropical fish, sharks, and turtles.
3. Khao Laem Ya - Mu Ko Samet National Park: Situated near Rayong City, this national park is known for its stunning coastal landscapes, including scenic viewpoints, pristine beaches, and hiking trails. You can hike to the top of Khao Laem Ya for panoramic views of the coastline or visit the park's islands, including the popular Koh Samet.
4. Fruit Orchards: Rayong Province is famous for its fruit orchards, and you can visit these orchards to experience the region's agricultural beauty. Durian, rambutan, mangosteen, and pineapple are some of the fruits grown in the area. You can taste fresh fruits, learn about the cultivation process, and enjoy the picturesque surroundings.
5. Temples and Cultural Sites: Rayong City has several temples and cultural sites worth exploring. Wat Pa Pradu, located in the city center, is a beautiful Buddhist temple known for

its large reclining Buddha statue. Wat Ban Kon Ao is another notable temple with intricate architectural details.
6. Seafood: Rayong is renowned for its fresh seafood, and you can indulge in delicious seafood dishes at the local restaurants and seafood markets. Try local specialties like grilled prawns, steamed fish, and seafood curries for a true culinary experience.
7. Festivals: Rayong City hosts various festivals throughout the year, celebrating local traditions and cultural heritage. The Rayong Fruit Festival, typically held in May, showcases the province's abundant fruit harvest with fruit parades, competitions, and food stalls. The Rayong Kite Festival, held in March, features colorful kite displays and competitions.

To reach Rayong City, you can travel by road from Bangkok or take a bus from Bangkok's Eastern Bus Terminal (Ekkamai) to Rayong. The journey takes approximately 2 to 3 hours, depending on traffic conditions.

Rayong City offers a mix of coastal beauty, cultural attractions, and culinary delights, making it a worthwhile destination for travelers looking to explore the eastern coast of Thailand.

Conclusion

Koh Samet is a captivating island in Thailand that offers pristine beaches, crystal-clear waters, and a relaxed atmosphere. Its convenient location, just a few hours from Bangkok, makes it a popular destination for both local and international visitors. Whether you're seeking a tranquil beach getaway, thrilling water sports, or vibrant nightlife, Koh Samet has something to offer.

The island's stunning beaches, such as Sai Kaew Beach, Ao Phai Beach, and Ao Wong Duean Beach, provide the perfect setting for sunbathing, swimming, and beach activities. You can also explore the island's natural beauty by hiking through its forests and discovering picturesque waterfalls.

Water sports enthusiasts will find plenty of options, including snorkeling, diving, kayaking, and jet skiing. The island's coral reefs offer a rich underwater world to explore, with colorful marine life and vibrant coral formations.

When it comes to dining, Koh Samet offers a variety of options. You can indulge in local cuisine and street food, savor fresh seafood, or dine at popular restaurants and cafes. The island's nightlife scene caters to different preferences, with beach bars, clubs, and live music venues where you can enjoy a vibrant atmosphere after sunset.

Accommodation options in Koh Samet range from luxury resorts and beachfront bungalows to budget-friendly guesthouses and backpacker accommodations. Whether you're looking for a romantic retreat, a family-friendly resort, or a budget-friendly stay, there's something to suit every preference and budget.

Koh Samet's local culture and festivals add an enriching dimension to your visit. You can learn about traditional Thai customs, participate in local celebrations, and witness the vibrant energy of festivals like Songkran (Thai New Year) and Loy Krathong (Festival of Lights).

Practical information, including weather conditions, currency exchange, safety tips, and healthcare facilities, should be considered when planning your trip. Additionally, the availability of communication and internet access ensures that you can stay connected during your stay.

For those who wish to explore beyond Koh Samet, the nearby islands of Koh Chang, Koh Kood, and other attractions in the Rayong area offer additional opportunities for adventure and discovery.

Overall, Koh Samet is a tropical paradise that combines natural beauty, outdoor activities, cultural experiences, and a laid-back beach vibe. Whether you're looking for relaxation, adventure, or a blend of both, Koh Samet is sure to leave you with lasting memories of your time in this captivating corner of Thailand.

Printed in Great Britain
by Amazon